Mind over Moment Journal

ANNE GRADY

Illustrated by Robyn Hedke

©2020 Anne Grady
www.annegradygroup.com
anne@annegradygroup.com
(512) 821-1111
PO Box 5815
Round Rock, TX 78683

All rights reserved. No part of this book may be used or reproduced by any means, graphic, electronic, or mechanical, including photocopying, recording, taping or by any information storage retrieval system without the written permission of the author except in the case of brief quotations embodied in critical articles and reviews.

Illustrated by Robyn Hedke
Cover design and interior by Brenda Hawkes

Printed in the United States of America

ISBN-13: 979-8679203501

Hello and welcome to the *Mind Over Moment Journal: Simple Reminders to Harness the Power of Resilience!*

This journal was born at one of my keynotes when teacher and illustrator Robyn Hedke showed me the sketch she made as she listened to my presentation. Inspiration struck, and I invited her to illustrate the essence of Mind Over Moment—the result is the journal you hold in your hands.

Practicing Mind Over Moment has taught me so much, and I want to share some of the daily practices I use with you. Journaling is a powerful way to reinforce and retain all the juicy tidbits in Mind Over Moment, and it provides an opportunity for reflection, intention setting, and accountability. It is a way to process and practice what you have learned so that you can apply the lessons in your own life.

You've read my story, now it's time to write your own! Record your hopes, dreams, and ambitions in these pages. Use the fun and whimsical reminders to help you live a life of purpose, on purpose.

You only get so many moments. Make yours count.

—Anne

What does your **Happily Ever After** look like?

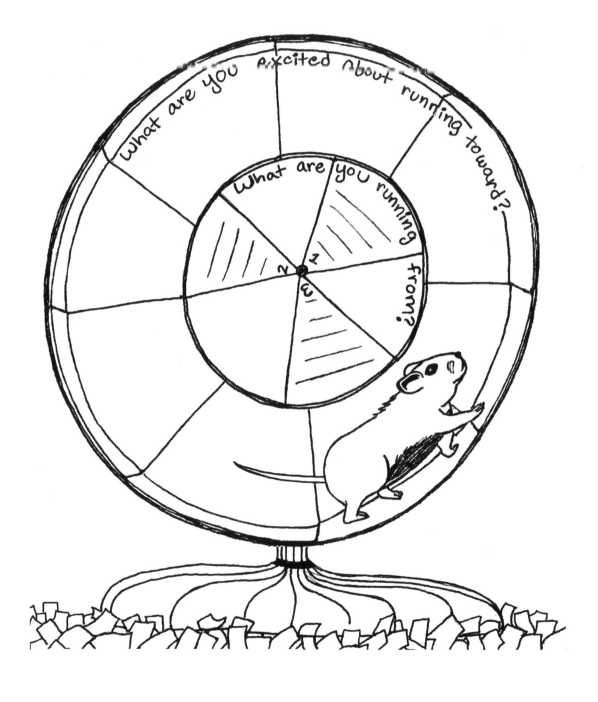

I have survived everything I have been through so far.
Here is what I learned.

Where in your life have you been *brave*, *resilient* and *strong?*

_____

_____

_____

_____

_____

_____

_____

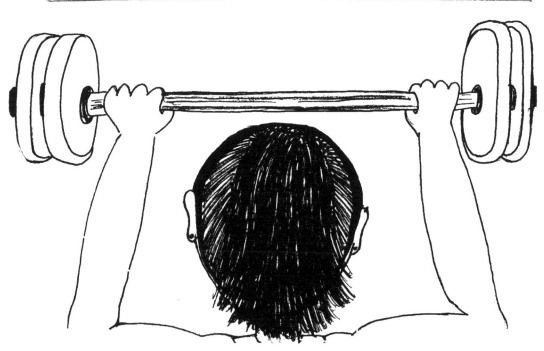

Make friends "with your" brain

What are realistic thoughts you can replace them with?

"I am getting better."

"I'm human. I make mistakes."

I am enough. I am human. I make mistakes. It didn't work this time, but I will keep trying. I get a lot of things right. I make a lot of good choices. I can do it again. Everyone needs help sometimes.

What negative, self-defeating thoughts are keeping you stuck?

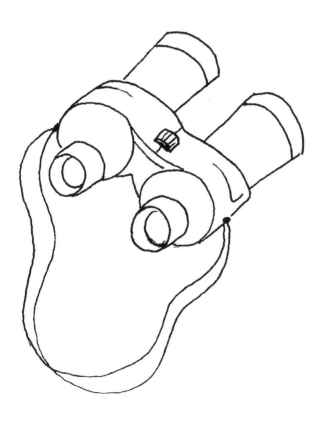

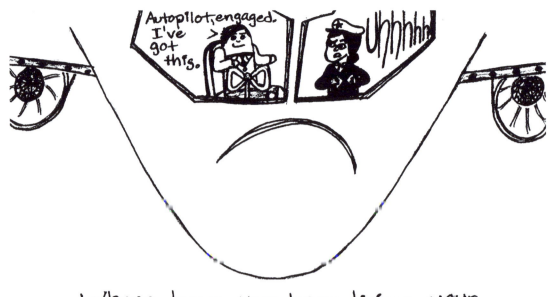

Where have you been living your life on auto-pilot? What's one small change you can make today to take back control?

_____
_____
_____
_____
_____
_____
_____
_____
_____
_____
_____
_____

daily habits

Identify 3 habits that <u>support</u> your success.
Identify 3 habits that <u>sabotage</u> your success.

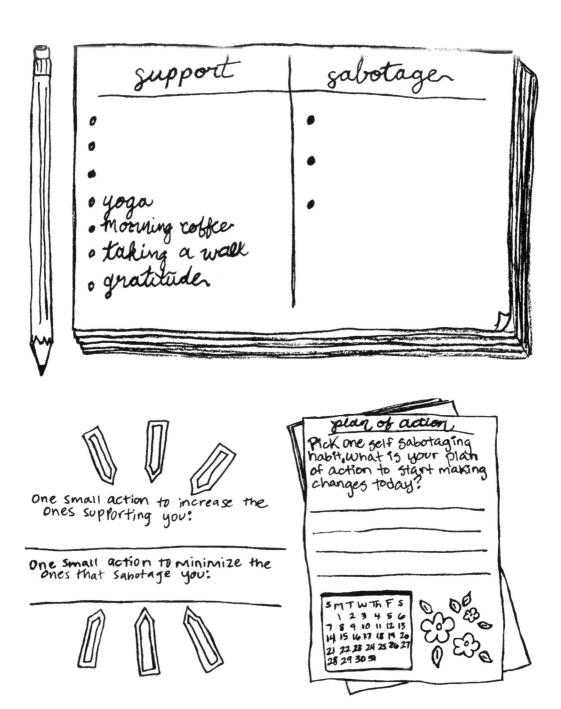

support	sabotage
○	●
○	
○	●
○ yoga	
○ morning coffee	●
○ taking a walk	
○ gratitude	

One small action to increase the ones supporting you:
_____

One small action to minimize the ones that sabotage you:
_____

plan of action
Pick one self sabotaging habit. What is your plan of action to start making changes today?
_____
_____
_____
_____

>> _____
>> _____
>> _____

>> _____
>> _____
>> _____

PICK 1
>> _____

what one action can you take to replace that habit with a more productive one?

Heya Habit!
Wish you weren't Here!

_____
_____
_____
_____
_____

Love,
♡ a better me ♡

What self limiting story are you telling yourself about yourself?

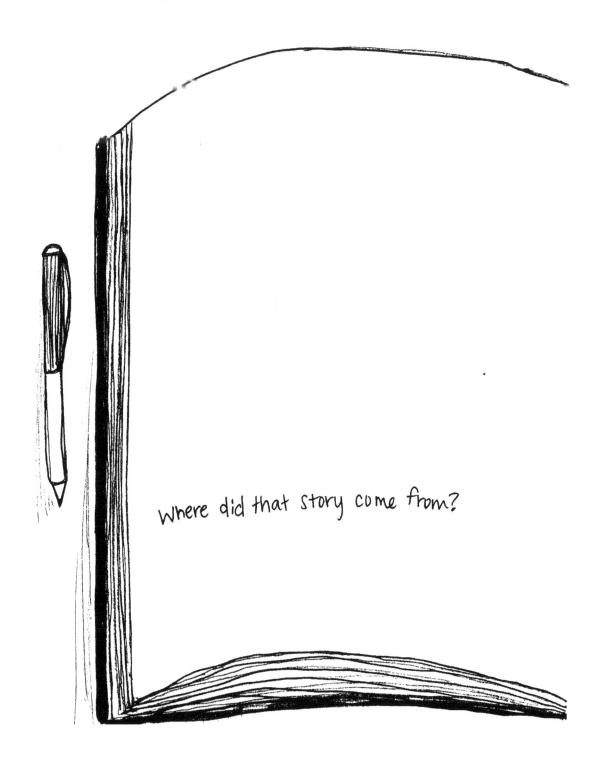

Where did that story come from?

How will you use Mind Over Moment to rewrite your story?

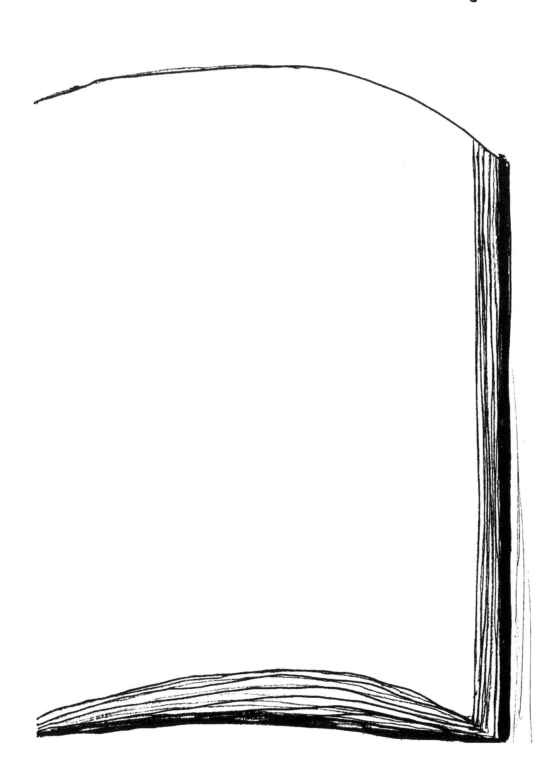

What have you told yourself you're not good at?

 STEPS toward a  GROWTH mindset

If <u>I get angry</u>, then <u>I will take 5 deep breaths before responding.</u>

| What are some of your If/Thens? |

If _____, then _____

If _____, then _____

If _____, then _____

Improve your ODDS of SUCCESS by having a specific plan.

Name your self-critical voice and draw it.

What will you do to get *unstuck*?

_____
_____
_____
_____
_____
_____
_____
_____

Take control of your day.
What can you do for the first 30 minutes instead of news, social media, and email?

What will you do for the last 30 minutes before you go to sleep?

Stress

is your body preparing itself, getting ready for action, putting on armor. This gives you time to make a plan of action and problem solve.
What do you do to handle stress and put on your armor?

What does your second shift look like?

What thoughts float through your mind at night?

Describe what courage means to you.

Draw your own definition of
Courage.

Emotional Management Process

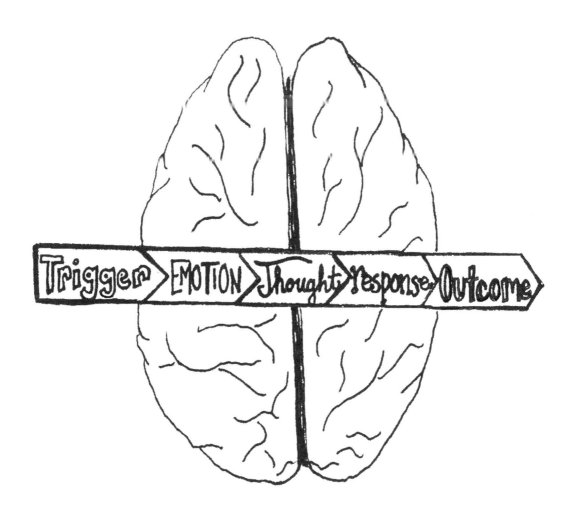

Create Your Own

Trigger _____

Emotion _____

Thought _____
_____

Response _____
_____

Outcome _____
_____

"Reframe the thought."

Thought
_____
_____
_____

Response
_____
_____

Outcome
_____
_____
_____

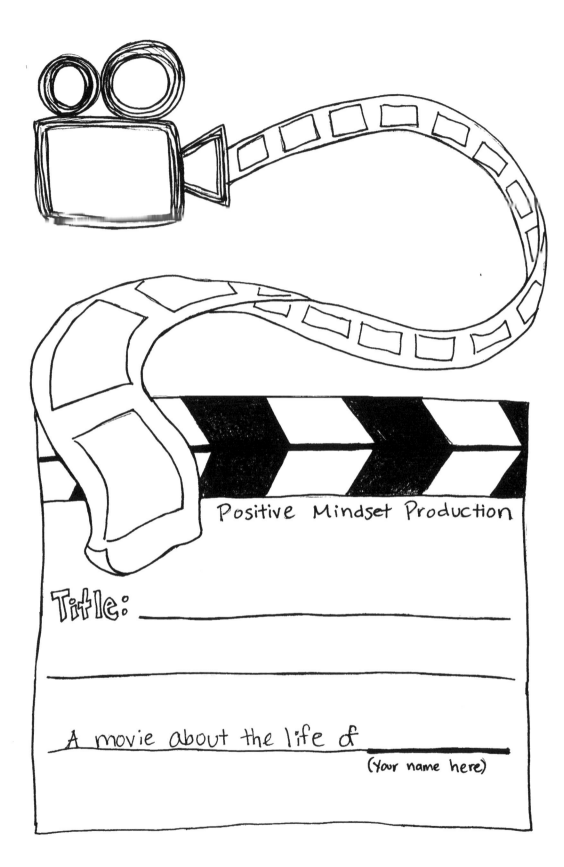

What will you do to remind yourself of all the ⓐⓜⓐⓩⓘⓝⓖ things you've done today?

Gratitude Prompts

Today I am grateful for _____
_____

I will text _____ to thank
them for _____.

I am excited about _____
_____.

I am proud of _____
_____.

I appreciate when people _____
_____.

What are you grateful for?

Think of a *delicious moments* you've experienced in the last 24 hours. Draw it.

How will you remind yourself to look for the positive?

What will go on your Delicious Moments board?

Laughter helps build RESILIENCE.

What has made you smile, giggle, or have a full blown belly laugh this week?

_____
_____
_____
_____
_____
_____
_____
_____
_____
_____
_____
_____
_____
_____

›› Humor Challenge

Record your funny experiences here.

How are you feeling at this moment?

 Name your emotion.

Where in your body do you feel it?

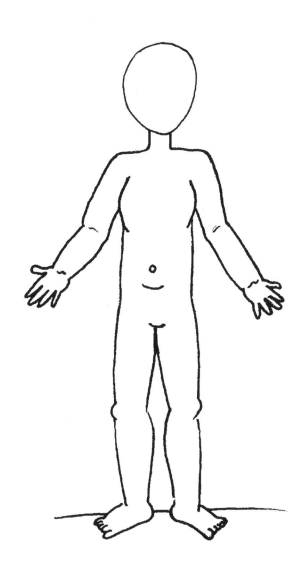

What positive things will you say to YOURSELF WHEN YOU Look in the mirror?

Random Acts of Kindness
What do you do to show kindness to others?

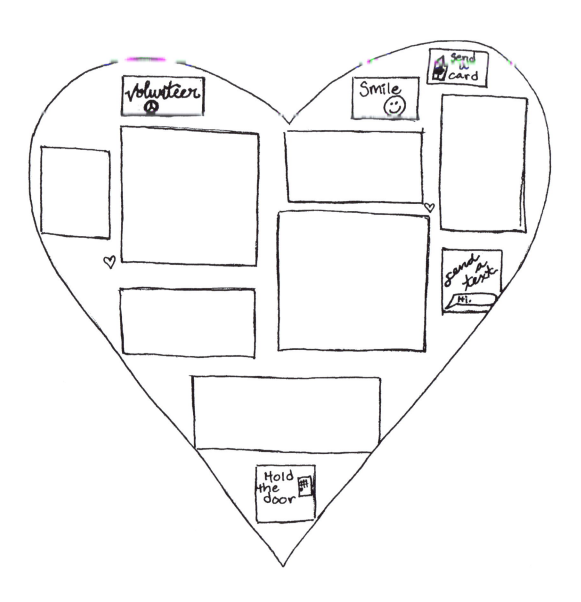

Perform one act of kindness each day this week.

Unplug and unwind

Draw
or
List
ways you practice self care.

Self Care
CHALLENGE

Identify one thing you can do each day this week to take care of yourself.

- M _____
- T _____
- W _____
- Th _____
- F _____
- S _____
- S _____

Who should you spend more time with? Who should you spend less time with?

_____

_____

_____

_____

_____

_____

_____

_____

Certificate for Kicking Ass

awarded for

_____

_____

_____

_____

actually cooked dinner

getting out of bed
when I didn't want to

everyone went
down for a nap

Made it to the gym and
went inside and didn't
have a soda at all today

called my boss
and said it was the best idea!

What will you look toward to keep yourself swimming in the *Right direction?*

Happiness is not a destination, it is a skill. What are 3 things that made you happy today?

1 _____

2 _____

3 _____

What is most important to you?

_____
_____
_____
_____
_____
_____
_____
_____
_____

Physical Health

1.
2.
3.

Family

1.
2.
3.

Mental Health

1.
2.
3.

Finances

1.
2.
3.

Social Life

1.
2.
3.

Career

1.
2.
3.

What are your most important priorities this week?

SUNDAY	
MONDAY	
Tuesday	
Wednesday	
T·H·U·R·S·D·A·Y	
Friday	
Saturday	

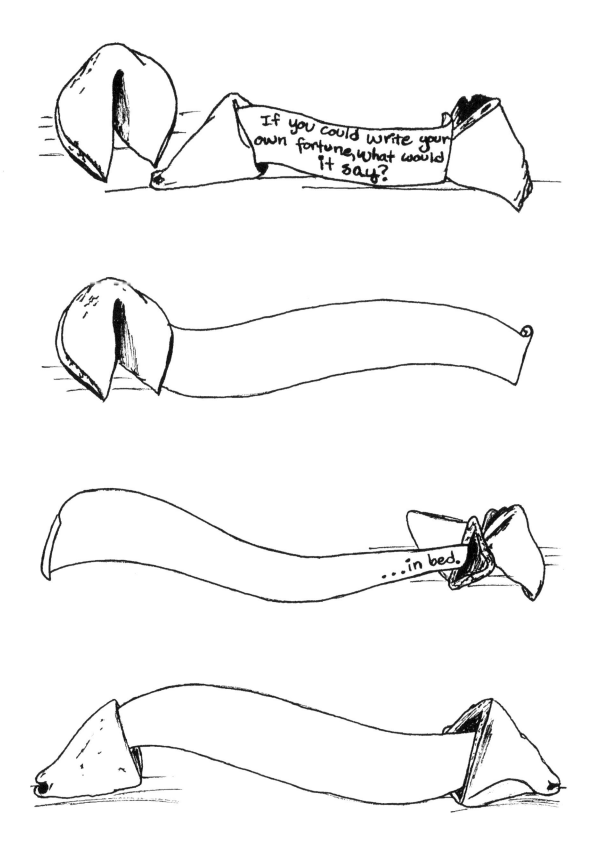

What do I want to be **remembered** for? What will I do to make my time here count?

I am strong enough.

Using Mind Over Moment, how will you keep building your resilience muscle?

Made in the USA
Monee, IL
24 April 2025

16323377R00081